MONTE OLIVETO MAGGIORE

the abbey born in a dream

THE FOUNDER

The founder of Mount Oliveto's Abbey and its Benedictine Congregation was born in Siena in 1272. He was baptised John and was educated as a nobleman of the *Tolomei* family.

At around the age of forty he felt called to more austere and penitent lifestyle. With some of his friends from Siena, who shared his ascetic ideal, he retired to an remote place, to the Southeast of Siena, among the clay rocks.

This land, known as *"Accona"*, was the property of the Tolomei family. When the monastery was founded, it was given the name of Mount Oliveto. John Tolomei changed his name to *Bernard*, in honour of the saint abbot from Clairvaux, and lived for several years as a hermit, though others followed his example. The number of people reaching the *"Accona's desert"* was

*Blessed
Bernard Tolomei.
Canvas (18th cent.)
by Stefano Pozzo
in the chapel
of the Grotto.*

*The vision
of the Silver Ladder.
Fresco (1780)
by Ermenegildo
Costantini
on the ceiling
of the church.*

steadily increasing when he had a supernatural vision. According to tradition, "one day, while Bernard was praying in the place where the church was later to be built, he saw a silver stairway rising eastwards, to Heaven. Jesus Christ and his Holy Mother, dressed in white, were standing at the top. A group of monks, all dressed in white, were climbing the stairs helped by angels" (*Chron.* by *Antonio da Barga*).

John Tolomei consulted the ecclesiastical diocesan authorities, since he and his friends wished to avoid being confused with the sects of friars who were opposing the Pope and his bishops.

Accona was part of the large Arezzo's diocese, under the control of bishop Guido Pietramala, who accepted Bernard's request that the *Benedictine Rule* be accepted. Bernard and his followers received the habit from him, together with the *Charta Fundationis* (26/3/1319) of the monastery of the Holy Virgin of Mount Oliveto, and the necessary authority to run the monastery.

As to the election of the abbot, the Blessed Bernard refused to be appointed, contrary to the general wish, so. In compliance with the abbey policy, which provided for annual appointments,

Patrick Patrizi, Bernard Tolomei and Ambrose Piccolomini. Fresco (15th cent.) over the side door of the choir.

St. Francis of Rome and the Angel. Canvas (17th cent.) of the side altar on the right.

three abbots were elected before him. During the Chapter of September 1321, he could no longer refuse to accept the appointment, which was confirmed every year until his death.

When, in 1348, the plague was spreading to Siena, Bernard returned to the town. He died among its victims, according to tradition on the 20th of August. He was subsequently venerated as a Saint and was officially recongnised (Beatified and his veneration authorised) in 1644. He is officially celebrated on August 19.

Outstanding among the ranks of the saints, together with Blessed Bernard, are around forty of his spiritual sons and daughters. Amongst whom the most celebrated is St. Frances of Rome, wife and mother, and afterwards foundress of the community of Tor de' Specchi in Rome.

*Portico
view
on Chiusure.*

BETWEEN "CRETE" AND INCENSE

Mount Olivet has the apperance of a great Benedictine Abbey. In a site solitary and wild in its natural state, it is a triumph of artistic beauty and spiritual peace. Situated on a hill, located near the geographical center of the dry and desolate wilderness of the Sienese *crete* within an area of about 215 acres, there sways a forest of cypresses, which together with pines, oaks, and olive trees form a superb park. On three sides, ravines and cliffs surround the abbey like a great wall. One approaches the monastery over a

*Tower and gate
of acces to the abbey
(16th cent.).*

*Madonna with Child
and St. Benedict.
Terracotta reliefs
by the Della Robbia school.*

drawbridge lonered from battlemented tower, from which a lovely Robbian Madonna seems to welcome you. When you leave, you will find in front of you on the opposite side of the tower the figure of the Patriarch of monks, St. Benedict, in a gesture of benediction, also from the school of the Della Robbia family.

Pretty little chapels, which the monks have dedicated to the greater saints of the Order, dot the immense greenery. In the center, flushed and majestic, rises the monastery, which also serves as, territorial

abbey, archabbey and mother-house of the congregation. To the side is the church with its imposing peaked campanile. On the square across the brick

Portico (16th. cent.).

*The abbey
seen from
Chiusure.*

road, you see the large building which once housed the ancient stables, and is now transformed into a pleasant guest house.

In the great cloister are celebrated the glories of St. Benedict by Signorelli and Sodoma. In oil paintings and frescoes scattered in various parts of the monastery, you will find extolled the greatness of the Virgin Mary, The Queen of the Olivetan institute.

The Choir by Fra Giovanni and the choral books illuminated by monks who humbly declined to be named a poem of prayer.

The library, though stripped of its past treasures, sings the poetry of study and of science.

If you follow me across the square in front of the church,

*The guest house,
with souvenir
stands.*

and into the large building, through the entrance door by the church.

Continuing past the recently, installed, through 15th century styled, wrought iron gate, you will find yourself in the great cloister, the artistic core of the monastery.

As you leave remember, by way of a last call, our shop is stocked with postcards, pictures, books, ceramics made by the monks, and delicate liqueurs prepared by the monks with aromatic herbs: FLORA, BITTER DROP, COFFEE ELIXIR, SAMBUCA; as well as *honey* and *oil* and other local products, and others coming from other Benedictine monasteries, such as *creams, ointments and herb teas, etc.*

Shops selling souvenirs and the monks' produce.

WHO ARE YOU?

We are Benedictine monks, and as such, our life is influenced not only by the WORD OF GOD, but also by ST. BENEDICT'S RULE and THE CONSTITUTIONS, which provide further details and practical information on the Rule. They also outline the structure and main features of our Congregation and its monasteries.

A Benedictine community is neither a business enterprise nor a club of devout

LET'S MEET THE MONKS

The porter's lodge.

The monks' life.
A picture.

The monastic community during the liturgy of the hours.

St. Benedict is explaining the rule to the novices.

believers.

It is rather like a big FAMILY, in which nobody has chosen the other members, who are considered as a gift of Our Lord, in order to reach Him all together.

The ABBOT (an ancient word, meaning "*father*") is the Superior of the monastery. Not only does he manage the monastery, but also plays a crucial role in the spiritual life of the community.

All monks, coming from different countries and of varying ages, are equal, sharing the same rights and duties.

They are frequently summoned by the Abbot (for the so-called "CHAPTERS"), in order to discuss different aspects of their lives, such as the admission of a new brother.

The novices are praying.

THE SWALLOW WHICH MADE A SUMMER: ST. BENEDICT

The life and works of St. Benedict, the founder of Western monasticism, have been described in "*The Dialogues*" by St. Gregory the Great. Benedict, born in Norcia in about 480 and educated in Rome, led the life of a hermit in a cave in Subiaco.

Several disciples followed his spiritual, cenobitical (or community) guidance. In 529 he reached Montecassino, where he wrote his famous RULE, summed up in the well-known saying "*ora et labora*". He is thought to have died on March 21, 547. St. Benedict is celebrated on the first spring day and on July 11 as the Protector of Europe, since his monks have supported European religious unity and fostered its cultural heritage.

St. Benedict. Mosaic (1980) by the Olivetan monk Ambrogio Fumagalli in the entrance hall.

The restorer's workshop for ancient books.

A TYPICAL MONKS' DAY

Monks' life perfectly balances "*ora et labora*" and study requirements, silence and brotherhood. The LITURGY of the Hours (when the Psalms are read or sung, in addition to other readings from the Bible) sequences the monastery day.

In our abbey, we usually meet in the Church choir six times (*Reading Office, Lauds and Third Hour, Noon and Rosary, None, Vespers and Conventual Mass, Compile*). Both in the morning and in the afternoon, the monks

Monks' cellar.

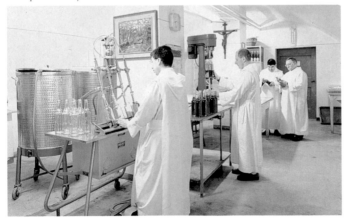

The liquor-distillery.

spend a great deal of time in HANDIWORKS.

They restore ancient books, produce liquors, perform agricultural or domestic tasks and also devote much time to personal prayers, to the "LECTIO DIVINA".

Monks eat breakfast, dinner and supper in silence, listening to instructional readings or classical and religious music.

HOW TO BECOME MONKS

To become a monk, young people (although you may enter the monastery at any age) must love God and praying, the core of our monastic life, although religious vocation may follow different paths.

After several stays at the abbey, in order to become familiar with everyday monastic life, the applicant fills in a written request for

Farm works.

admission to the POSTULATION PERIOD, lasting about one year, during which the community and the candidate himself will investigate whether his vocation is true and the candidate genuine.

He will well wear the HABIT, to start one year of NOVITIATE, at the end of which he will be able to make the TEMPORARY PROFESSION OF VOWS.

His commitment is confirmed after at least three years, with the PERPETUAL (i.e. final) PROFESSION.

At the beginning, several years are devoted to the study of theological topics, which could be useful to the young postulant should he be chosen as priest by the Abbot, provided he has the necessary qualifications.

HOSPITALITY

Hospitality is a well-known and recognised traditional value of Benedictine monasteries.

We put our large GUEST-ROOMS at the disposal of both individuals and families, who must book in advance with the Hospitaller.

We hope our abbey will always be, as in the past, a place of harmony, faith, culture and art.

To this end, every year we use to plan a variety of successful and well attended events, such as conventions, meetings, seminars and interdisciplinary debates.

A monk during LECTIO DIVINA.

MOUNT OLIVETO:
ONE HEART
FOR MANY SONS

To foster the monastic movement which spontaneously developed around Mount Oliveto's Abbey, Clement VI canonically set up the BENEDICTINE CONGREGATION OF ST. MARY OF MOUNT OLIVETO on January 21, 1344.

The Congregation quickly developed, although it was confined to Italy.

The number of monasteries (ten in 1344) grew to 23 in collapse of 1797, with the Cisalpine Republic and the general decree of dissolution of Religious Orders (1808), imposed at various intervals. However, the Congregation did not disappear, being ready to develop again in the late 19th century (1875), in a small monastery at Settignano (Florence).

Many saints belonged to the Congregation over the centuries.

Besides St. Bernard and St.

The venerable Abbot is talking to a monk.

1400, with new foundations extending outside the regions (Tuscany, Umbria, Latium) where this religious movement had originally developed. 76 monasteries were built in the 16th century, which would grow to 82 in the following century.

Suppression began in the late 18th century, in the Venetian Republic (1771), in Lombardy, in the Grand Duchy of Tuscany, until the Frances from Rome, its monks were famous in several artistic fields (miniature, inlaying, painting, sculpture, music and literature).

The Benedictine habit is white, in honour of the Holy Virgin.

At present, the Congregation has a variety of abbeys and prioral churches in Italy, France, United Kingdom, Ireland, Israel, Korea, USA, Mexico, Guatemala, Brazil.

*The bell-tower
from the great Cloister.*

THE GREAT CLOISTER

The great cloister so named to distinguish it from the two smaller ones that follow it, known respectively as the middle cloister and the little cloister. These two lesser cloisters are marked by the *clausura*. On climbing the stairway to the library in the middle cloister one observes a mixed severity and playfulness in its lines. The little cloister, more poetic and suffused with a mystical light pouring down from the tall building that enlocks it, is part of the living quarters of the monks.

The great cloister is the wonder of Mount Olivet. Constructed in three periods from 1426 to 1443, and under three Abbots General, Andrea Bettini of Bologna, Lorenzo Marsupini of Arezzo and Francesco Ringhieri of Bologna, the architecture does not offer that regularity that would have been expected in a block construction. Some arches are wide, some narrow; there are a greater number on the north side than on the south. But, on the whole, these are matters of little concern. Beautiful and solemn in the huge wrought-iron windows that enclose it on all four sides, it offers a superb setting for the frescoes of *Luca Signorelli* and ANTONIO BAZZI CALLED SODOMA.

*The gallery
of the great Cloister
on the first floor.*

GREAT
CLOISTER

The great Cloister, the well.

The Abbot General was truly inspired when he called these great masters to transform this cloister into one of the most splendid jewels Italian painting can boast.

The works was were realized during the two terms in which Abbot Domenico Airoldi of Lecco held office as Superior General of the Olivetan Congregation. It was he who summoned Signorelli in 1495 and Sodoma in 1505. They left a legacy the likes of which one does not find in the cloisters of such renowned abbeys as Monte Cassino, Subiaco, Praglia, Camaldoli and Vallombrosa. The theme of the frescoes is the life (f St. Benedict, in its most significant episodes, as related by *St. Gregory the Great* in the second book of this *Dialogues*. Signorelli, called first to the gigantic labor, took as his point of departure a few episodes of the adult life of St. Benedict. Sodoma, second to the task, began at the most significant episode of the Saint's youth. Faithfully following the events according to their chronological order, he worked up to che series of stories already celebrated by the brush of his great predecessor, overtaking and completing them with other episodes. History does not tell us the reason for this inversion in the work of the two artists. Don Luigi M. Perego, in his *Guida Illustrata di Monte Oliveto Maggiore*, states his opinion that the reason may be found in the possible pre-existence of paintings on the section now illustrated by the frescoes of Sodoma; for in the year 1474, according to the Olivetan historian Besozzi, a certain Master Mariano di Matteo was summoned from Rome to paint in Mount Olivet. To him we may attribute the figures of hermits painted on the inside of the cloister pillars and painted over in the eighteenth century by Solimena of Naples. Some of the original figures have been brought back to light. Of others, one can see portions, of the monks' habits beneath the more recent paintings by Solimena, which are gradually disappearing.

Chronologically, our tour of the great cloister of Mount Olivet should begin with Signorelli's first fresco, but practically, it would be better to begin with Sodoma's first, which is the first historically in the life of St. Benedict. We shall give brief historical and descriptive notes on each composition. In order to be understood correctly, let me remark that the figures and the various actions should be considered not from their wall position, but in their position relative to the spectator.

If you enter from the church, you will find the first fresco immediately on your left as you pass the arch that opens into the cloister. If, instead, you come in through the main entrance, you will find it at the end of the frescoed corridor which opens immediately to your left as you leave the entrance hall.

Gallery of the great Cloister with frescoes by Sodoma.

ST. BENEDICT CONFERS
THE RULE ON THE
OLIVETAN MONKS

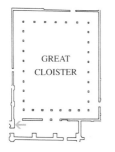

GREAT
CLOISTER

The painting is a symbolic representation of the inclusion of the Congregation of Mount Olivet into the sphere of Benedictine monasticism through St. Benedict's Rule, in that Bernard Tolomei did not give his Congregation its own Rule, but that of the Patriarch of Western Monasticism.

Even a layman can comprehend that the faces, the draperies and the style make it a painting by Sodoma.

On the abbatial seat Benedict, majestic and paternal in his white cowl and particulary in the broad gesture of his arms, offers two copies of his Rule to two monks, who are surrounded by their companions. Beneath, a Latin inscription recording the beginning of the Olivetan Congregation on the 26th day of March 1319, the Supreme Pontiff being John XXII.

This fresco shows Benedict in the commotion of a first separation: that from his parents and little sister, Scholastica. He demonstrates, in perfect accord with the historical narrative, the flowering of a refined and healthy youth, as befitting a descendant of Roman proconsuls. He is mounted on an able charger, which he commands with a sure hand even in the tender gesture of a last farewell. His eyes, lightly tinged with red, and his body bent towards the group of relatives, could not better express his delicate love and the sadness of the separation. So too, the sorrowful expression of the faces of the bystanders. The identification of Benedict's mother can be made from the marked likeness between his face and that of the woman of the left foreground standing near his

How Benedict Leaves Home And Goes To Study In Rome

GREAT CLOISTER

father. Both mother and father, in a gesture of farewell, betray signs of emotion. The woman sitting on the mule can be none other than the reliable nurse, Cyrilla, who will accompany the lad, and of whom St. Gregory tells us in his narrative. Graceful is the detail of the little girl whose dog is biting her skirt is particulary graceful and comical is that of the two donkeys with the driver drinking from a flask.

Notice that one of the donkeys is missing its forelegs. The colourfully dressed youth, his agile body bent forward prepared to run, and his head turned to assure himself of being followed, is shown to be an excellent guide. The background of Benedict's native Norcia, imaginatively depicted on a hill, and the country-side, furrowed by a river, give the composition breadth and serenity.

How Benedict leaves home and goes to study in Rome; detail.

HOW BENEDICT LEAVES THE SCHOOL IN ROME

Benedict's schooling in Rome has revealed to him the dangers of a hedonistic and epicurean education, and the vices of a society as morally corrupt as in the most depraved pagan centuries. To remain there would mean drinking of that poison and placing himself on the road to moral perdition. A mysterious voice told him that only the rigorous life of the wilderness and the meditation of the Sacred

Scriptures will instill within him the force to resist. The command of this voice is so strong and sure, that Benedict abandons once and for all the school to which his parents had sent him.

Sodoma depicts the youth at the very moment of this resolute departure. He has conceived of the school in the Greek fashion: a porticoed hall, the stern rector on his throne in the center reading

off his thoughts, the pupils on either side. To the left, Hadrian's tomb and the Tiber give the view breadth and expansion. The features, the apparel and the attitudes of the students tell you that you are looking at a group cosmopolitan in instinct, taste and ideals. And if the face of the lad just beginning his studies speaks of a cheerful restlessness, that of the older man shows reflections, and that of a third figure betrays a vulgar and licentious spirit.

Benedict's figure is Leonardian in the manly delicacy of this face, encircled by chestnut-colored hair. The movement of the figure gives it realism and a life. Does he not appear as though he were detaching himself a live from the wall and walking off? The three *putti* on the architrave add a graceful note.

HOW BENEDICT LEAVES THE SCHOOL IN ROME

GREAT CLOISTER

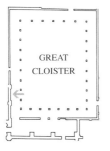

HOW BENEDICT
MENDS THE CRIBBLE
THAT WAS BROKEN

GREAT
CLOISTER

In the same fresco we have two apparently unrelated scenes. They are connected, however, like the stanzas of a single song. Standing to the left, disconsolate, is a woman. A large wooden tray has fallen from her hand and broken into two pieces. Next to her on his knees, with his hands joined and an ecstatic expression on his face is Benedict, rapt in prayer. Before him is the mended tray. To understand this episode, we must recall, that after having left school in Rome and withdrawn to a life of prayer and penance, Benedict, before reaching the solitude of Mount Subiaco, lived for some time in a little town called Affile. The nurse, Cyrilla, both for the grave responsability with which she felt burdened, as well as for the affection she bore Benedict, would not permit him to go off alone under any circumstances. And so she too went along, remaining with him throughout this whole period and continuing her maternal calling. Now it happened, relates St. Gregory the Great, that as Cyrilla had some grain to clean, she borrowed a cribble from a neighboring peasant woman. The object, however, fell from her hand and broke. The woman began to weep, and Benedict to comfort her prayed to God, and the cribble was mended. In the face of an angel is that of Benedict. There is an expression of the most genuine sorrow in the face and in the movement of the nurse. Every detail of the scene is eminently true to life. On the other side of the pillar, a cavalier and a group of people look in awe at the cribble, which is now hanging on the front of a church. This is the sequel to the episode in St. Gregory's narrative; for since the people of the vicinity had come to learn of the prodigy, they had hung the tray over the church entrance as a perpetual memorial. In the cavalier, Sodoma has portrayed himself; in the group, supposedly, his relatives. The anachronism of the medieval garb he is wearing has its historical explanation in the fact that a gentleman from Milan had recently received the monastic habit, and since the Abbot General had given the novice's mantle to Sodoma, the latter thought to portray himself with it on. The animals at the artist's feet are his favorite. The composition as a whole and the distibution of its parts, Sodoma's eloquent expression and the life throbbing in the flesh of the first two figures of the group, place this fresco among the most perfect of the cycle.

Self-portrait of Sodoma.

How the monk Romanus gives Benedict the hermit's habit

GREAT CLOISTER

The old, austere monk who is giving Benedict, reverently kneeling at his feet, a habit similar to the one he himself is wearing is that Romanus mentioned by St. Gregory.

His head is strikingly realistic and powerful. In Benedict, everything speaks of refinement and grace. We find the logical and historical connection between this fresco and the preceding one in Benedict, who, dressed in the garb of a young Roman and with a determined pace, appears in the background on the left. The wild landscape of the area and the mountainous background to the city of Subiaco give the scene a note of marked harshness. The peristyle of the church with a monk meditating over a book brings to mind the monastery of Romanus, as well as the many others which Benedict will build in Subiaco himself. Of Virgilian aspect is the detail of the two shepherds, one of them plucking the strings of a mandolin while their sheep graze nearby. It is a pity the fresco is damaged in spots.

This unusual incident has been created by Sodoma on the fresco with only two brush strokes: on the upper left, the devil hurling the stone with one stroke, and the breaking of the bell with the other.

On Benedict's face, no longer framed by the long flowing hair of the previous frescoes and already darkened by a sprouting beard, there is a note of devout energy. The ample folds of the monastic cowl, the fissures in the rock, as well as the coloring of the wild landscape blend together in a remarkable unity. The boats on the lake, the trees on the mountainside and the little church all alleviate the harshness of the cave.

HOW THE DEVIL BREAKS THE BELL

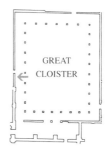

GREAT CLOISTER

HOW A PRIEST, INSPIRED BY GOD, BRINGS BENEDICT FOOD ON EASTER DAY

GREAT CLOISTER

This is the page of introduction to a voluminous book which Benedict will write with his own hand, namely the progressive affirmation of the great destiny to which God has called him; for it is with this fresco that we begin to realize that Benedict's destiny is not that of a hermit, however great and noble that calling may be. The story we shall shortly witness will present him to us as leading a common life with many other men, in the capacity of superior and for the realization of a program of religion and civilization. This fresco depicts the man whom Providence used to recover the "hermit". He is a charitable and pious priest of the area. The day, for Christians, is one of the greatest feasts of the year, Easter Sunday.

As a servant prepares the food with the great abundance usual on feast days, Christ appears to the priest and reveals Benedict's hiding place to him, with the command that he bring a portion of that food to him. Promptly and cheerfully, the priest carries out the order. Even with the adaptation imposed by the window, the fresco depicts the two parts of the one episode with realism and artistic brilliance. To the right is the priest, who, in response to the mysterious voice, looks up towards the window, through which there pours a mystical light and above which is the Redeemer. Behind the priest in the room is the servant preparing the dinner.

Notice how the priest, to shield his eyes from the blinding light, covers his brow with his right hand. The servant has his left hand raised to defend himself from the great heat, and his right hand intent on the work.

To the left is the completion of the episode. Benedict, an expression of gratitude on his face, is seated at the table prepared for him by the Providence of God and the charity of a brother. The priest kneeling before Benedict has a look of admiration and regret, as if he has arrived too late or as if the food brought is too poor. The servant mixing the wine speaks of the freshness of youth. Note the details of the table, the basket on the ground, and the portraits of two monks in the tondos of the window.

*Detail
of the scene
on the left.*

HOW BENEDICT INSTRUCTS
VISITING PEASANTS
IN SACRED DOCTRINE

This is the first public manifestation of the Benedictine *Labora*, and a foreshadowing of the work that Benedict and his spiritual offspring were to accomplish. For, not only will they harrow uncultivated countrysides and there sow the grain for their daily bread, but having become teachers to all nations with the preaching of the gospel, they would lead man back on the path of that Christian civilization which was being eroded by barbarism and dissolution. Benedict, his bearing dignified, inspirational and noble, is portrayed in the act of counting on his fingers in order to clarify some point of his teaching. The group of peasants, is so varied and so realistic, with their attentive faces, their manner of dress and bearing. Note the splendid young shepherd leaning on his staff, his legs crossed, his shirt torn at the shoulder and the dog at his feet.

Our historian, St. Gregory, relates that one day Benedict felt whithin him a temptation of the flesh so violent as he had never before experienced.

Evil phantasms so perturb his imagination and his senses that he is on the verge of declaring himself unable to lead a life of perfect continence, and of making the decision to return to that way of life in which even the flesh may have its legitimate pleasures.

Benedict is seated with the abandon of one nearly vanquished. With one hand supporting his head, weighed down, as it were, by the impure temptation, and the other with fingers stretched out as though reaching for assistance, he marvellously expresses the gravity of the battle being waged within him.

HOW BENEDICT,
TEMPTED TO IMPURITY,
OVERCOMES THE TEMPTATION

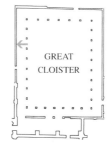

GREAT
CLOISTER

Above, the artist has imaginatively, represented the temptation. The evil spirit, in the form of a woman in transparent veils, casts one last languid glance of seduction at Benedict. The Archangel Michael, however, appears to drive away the seducer.

On the lower right, Benedict has thrown himself unclothed into a bramble bush. It is this deed, more effective than any other weapon, that has secured for his flesh its triumph over the lustful demon.

*How Benedict,
tempted to impurity,
overcomes
the temptation; detail.*

This fresco portrays Benedict receiving a group of hermits

from the vicinity, who have come to ask him to be their superior. In the distance is their hermitage. The landscape, though varied, still bears the tonality of that of the previous composition. The hermits, on their knees before Benedict, seem to be thanking him for the burden he has assumed. Benedict, already prepared to follow them, shows the fullness of manhood and ability to command.

HOW BENEDICT, AT THE ENTREATY OF CERTAIN HERMITS, CONSENTS TO BE THEIR SUPERIOR AND ABBOT

GREAT CLOISTER

HOW BENEDICT, WITH THE SIGN OF THE CROSS, BREAKS A GLASS OF POISONED WINE

GREAT CLOISTER

This is the episode of the first attempt against Benedict's life. The instigator is the devil, who fears the survival of a man resolutely dedicated to the reflourishing of Christian life and civilization. His unhappy agents are the hermits of the previous fresco. St. Gregory relates that as the monks were extremely lax and heedles of the rules, Benedict began reproaching them, at first gently, and then more forcefully. Intolerant, however, of every reproof, they decide to get rid of him by offering him a glass of poisoned wine. Providence saves Benedict, however, causing the glass to break at the sign of the cross.

A great portrait of human psychology is depicted in the faces, variously angry and contracted are those of the hermits, as well as their gestures. An understandable

indignation, as well as Christian forgiveness is seen in Benedict's face.

Notice some of the hermits preparing the poisoned drink at the end of the corridor behind the departing Benedict.

*The hermits preparing
the poisoned drink; detail.*

Detail of the scene on the left.

HOW BENEDICT COMPLETES THE CONSTRUCTION OF TWELVE MONASTERIES

GREAT CLOISTER

Before us stands not only the Patriarch of Western monasticism, but also the architect of the first Benedictine monasteries. Benedict, his noble body erect, has his head lifted up towards the scaffolding and his mouth open in giving directions, which he clarifies by means of the rod raised in his right hand. From the scaffolding, the bricklayer has interrupted his work, and his leaning over with his head turned in order to hear the instruction. Behind Benedict two monks look on. Under the already finished arches, the painter goes about his work with a long feather-topped pole. Energetic and full of life is the stonecutter with his arm raised in his labor. A young artisan monk has suspended his work and is listening to the observations of an onlooker.

This is one of the best and one of the most grandiose of Sodoma's frescoes. Arriving from Rome, accompanied by their respective fathers and retinue, are Maurus and Placid, two young boys who will be Benedict's two most valuabue collaborators in the works he has undertaken.

The eye fixed in meditation can sense and conceive more than the pen the infinite beauty that comes to light from the observation of each subject and of the composition as a whole. The youthful figures of Maurus and Placid and of the three lads encircling them have a Raphaelesque delicacy and grace. Most venerable is the figure and fatherly attitude of Benedict. We note the melancholy of a sorrowful separation of the Leonardian faces of the two fathers, Equitius and Tertullus. There is naturalness and variety in

HOW BENEDICT RECEIVES THE TWO BOYS FROM ROME, MAURUS AND PLACID

the variety, in the bearing, movement and style of dress of the entourage, made up, as it is, of persons of every race and color.

In the background, the landscape has some beautiful Roman monuments, and under the solemn triumphal arch, a shining cavalcade of soldiers, whose rear guard is seen in the distance.

How benedict receives the two boys from Rome, Maurus and Placid; detail.

This fresco shows wholesome punishment inflicted on a monk who, while his confrères were at prayer, had yielded to a caprice and gone off for a stroll. The temptation is symbolized by the small dark creature who takes hold of the restless monk by a fold of his habit and invites him to come out. The scene is subdivided into three parts. Benedict at prayer, with his eyes follows the young monk whom the seducer is pulling out by his habit. The same Benedict has caught up with the monk outside the curch, and is scourging him on his bared back until be begins to bleed. Under the little triangular pavilion, the monk on his knees receives Benedict's pardon. In the clouds the devil, writhing, flees. On the terrace, we see a monk reading and another monk holding a purse, a figure this latter of the administrator. Hurried and careless as the work is, it has on the whole ingeniousness and life.

How Benedict delivers a possessed monk by scourging him

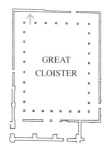

GREAT CLOISTER

HOW BENEDICT, ENTREATED
BY THE MONKS, PRODUCES
WATER FROM THE TOP
OF THE MOUNTAIN

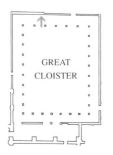

GREAT
CLOISTER

The eight monks kneeling before Benedict have come to address a fervent petition to their good Father. On the mountain, where three monasteries already rise on as many cliffs, there is not even one fountain. Going down every day to the lake below to draw essential water is a difficult and dangerous undertaking. If Benedict wishes habitation on the hill to continue, he must in some way provide.

Benedict has affectionately heard the petition, and dismisses the monks with words of comfort and hope. «The following night», continues St. Gregory, «Benedict climbs the mountain and after having prayed with fervour, marks the spot with three stones and returns to the monastery. The next day, to the distressed monks on their return, he says: «Go up to the cliff. There you will find three stones one on top of the other.

Dig a little and almighty God, if it be His Will, may give you the water you desire». And so it was. The single episode shows in this fresco, besides the main incident of the monks presenting their plea, two secondary ones showing. St. Benedict's prayer and the finding of water. We might mention that for this act St. Benedict would be compared to Moses, who with the touch of his rod made water spring forth from a stone. On top to the right under the monastery is Benedict in prayer with a monk. A little below, the monks have struck water which has already begun to flow. An animal is thirstily drinking on the slope. Although this fresco too is flawed by its carelessness, there is a great deal of grace and variety in the well-modelled faces. Angelic are those of the young, austerely devout those of the older.

The eight monks kneeling; detail.

This composition is dominated by the figure of Benedict on his knees, bent over the waters of the lake of Subiaco. He immerses the long handle of the hedging bill that has slipped off during work and fallen into the lake. At Benedict's side, also kneelling, his face contracted with sorrow, his left hand over his breast and the index finger of his right hand held out over the lake, is the monk who has lost the blade of his hedging bill.

He is a monk descended from those barbarians, who under the name of Goths, Visigoths and Ostrogoths, put Italy to sack and sword. St. Gregory, our historian, gives him the generic name of Goth. It would not be out of place to mention here the work of civilization carried on in Benedictine monasteries by these barbarian elements. Fused and merged in with those of Latin descent, they no longer pose a danger, but have become, instead, an effective aid in actuating the program of recivilizing Europe.

Miraculously, St. Gregory relates, and as though in response to a friendly voice, the blade came up to insert itself back onto its handle, and Benedict returned the tool back to the Goth with the words:«Here, work and be sad no longer».To the left two details of lesser importance and earlier in chronological order. The Goth, surprised and dismayed, looks at the long handle deprived of its blade; higher up, the Goth, humble and sad, relates the loss to Benedict. The monk near him is Maurus. Sodoma's bizarre humour has its part here too. Over the lake on the right, he has depicted a group of bathers engaged in a boxing bout and otherwise variously amusing themselves. Peter the Deacon, commenting on this episode, compare St. Benedict to the prophet Eliseus.

The Goth, humble and sad, relates the fact to Benedict.

This incident is so realistically portrayed, that the figures seem to talk and move.

It happened, relates St. Gregory, that the monk Placid had gone to draw water from the lake, had fallen in and was close on drowning. Benedict, who has miraculously had a vision of what was happening, calls Maurus and orders him to run and save Placid. Upheld by a mysterious power, Maurus walk on the waves and draws Placid back to safety. To the right, Maurus with a gentle effort saves the drowning boy. The face of Placid, who is holding on to his rescure's habit, shows a trusting resignation.

An errand-boy, sent to bring Benedict two large flasks of wine, allows himself to be overcome by greediness along the way. «After all» he says to himself, «he does not know whether the owner has given me two flasks, or only one. I will bring him just one; the other I will hide in this hedge and bring home myself». And the boy did just that. With only one flask of wine, he presents himself before Benedict, who accepts the offering and thanks him benevolently. He promptly adds, however:«Be careful not to drink from the flask you have hidden, but first make sure of what it contains». The youth, shamed, goes and finds the flask he had hidden, but as soon as he places his hand on it, he draws it back, horrified on seeing a livid serpent emerge from the bottle. The episode, which is narrated by St. Gregory in the eighteenth chapter of the Dialogues is here portrayed in two parts. To the

HOW BENEDICT CHANGES INTO A SERPENT THE FLASK OF WINE HIDDEN FROM HIM BY AN ERRAND-BOY

GREAT CLOISTER

*How Benedict
changes into a serpent
the flask
of wine hidden
from him by an errand-boy;
detail showing St. Benedict
and the errand-boy.*

left, the boy reverently offering the flask of wine, with Benedict's thanks and warning; to the right, the finding of the flask with the snake emerging from it. Notice for their particular comeliness the figure of the errand-boy before St. Benedict, as well as the head of the monk behind him. The figure of St. Benedict, coarse and hard, shows so much carelessness and deficiency as to permit its attribution to another painter or to a rebellious intent on the part of Sodoma himself.

Here we have the pictorial narration of the second attempt on Benedict's life, which is once again saved by a divine inspiration. The evil protagonist is an unworthy priest named Florentius, who sends Benedict a loaf of poisoned bread. Our historian makes the motive behind this attempt on Benedict's life consist in the priest's envy of the great reputation which the man of God had earned for himself with his sanctity, and also in the depravation of his corrupt heart, which while hearing Benedict's continual reproach against his irregular life, would not make the least effort to reform. God, however, comes to the aid of His servant. Mysteriously forewarned, Benedict throws the loaf to a domesticated crow with the command that it carry it far away so that no one might eat of it.

HOW FLORENTIUS TRIES TO POISON BENEDICT

GREAT CLOISTER

*How Florentius
sends evil women
to the monastery;
detail of the group
of young women.*

Sodoma has arranged the episode within the framework of a magnificent arcade, and to give us at first glance an idea of the already discovered deception, he depicts Benedict with unusual severity. In the center with the monks is Benedict receiving the loaf. To the right, he has firmly refused it and thrown it to the crow. To the left in front of the little church is Florentius, delivering the instrument of his crime to a servant. In every phase of the episode, the various characters throb with life and profound realism.

Continuing the story, Sodoma places us before two groups of people who, though poles apart one from the other in their way of life, are here brought together by the malice of an unworthy and vulgar man who is seeking the monks perdition. To the right, a group of spirited young women, their movements, and their glances, a fascinating display of feminine grace. Four are stepping to a dance. To the left, a group of monks departing with St. Benedict for an unknown destination. In an arch of the upper portico on the right, two figures are accompanying the dance with music and song. The monk on the balcony to the left, observing everything with indignation, is Benedict himself, who after mature counsel will decide on the departure immortalized in the fresco.

GREAT CLOISTER

*How Florentius
sends evil women
to the monastery;
detail of St. Benedict and
his monks leaving
the monastery.*

On this attempt to destroy Benedict's work, Divine Providence will make use for the foundation of Monte Cassino. The diabolical protagonist is the already mentioned Florentius who, narrates St. Gregory, disappointed in his first attempt on Benedict, sends seven young women to dance under the monastery, in the hope that the seduction of pleasure might succeed where poison has failed.

The composition is considered a masterpiece. It is the last in the series of frescoes by Sodoma, which although painted after those of Signorelli, depict a preceeding era.

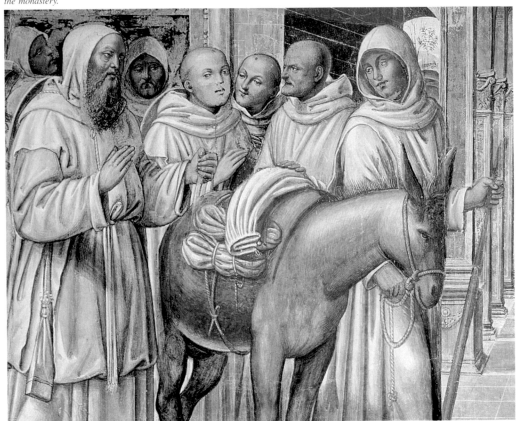

HOW BENEDICT SENDS MAURUS TO FRANCE AND PLACID TO SICILY

This fresco is the anticipation of an event which chronologically ought to follow.

For the departure of Maurus for France and Placid for Sicily on their mission of evangelization took place after the events which Signorelli immortalized in

the following frescoes. Placid's departure, in fact, took place about the year 537, that of Maurus about the year 546. The episode depicted in the next fresco, however, takes place in the year 528.

It goes without saying that this fresco has nothing in common with either the previous or the subsequent compositions. It is from the brush of Bartolomeo Neroni called Riccio, Sodoma's son-in-law.

It depicts St. Benedict giving the Rule to Maurus (to his right) and Placid (to his left), as they leave on their mission of evangelization.

The character to the left of Maurus represents the King of France, Maurus's destination, and it is believed to be a self-portrait of the painter.

HOW BENEDICT SENDS MAURUS TO FRANCE AND PLACID TO SICILY

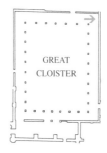

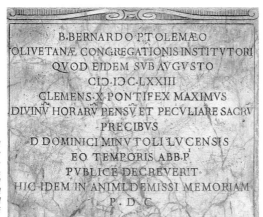

B.BERNARDO P.TOLEMÆO
OLIVETANÆ CONGREGATIONIS INSTITVTORI
QVOD EIDEM SVB AVGVSTO
CIƆ.IƆC.LXXIII
CLEMENS·X·PONTIFEX MAXIMVS
DIVINV̅ HORARV̅ PENSV̅ ET PECVLIARE SACRV̅
·PRECIBVS
D·DOMINICI MINVTOLI LVCENSIS
EO TEMPORIS ABB.P
PVBLICE DECREVERIT·
HIC·IDEM IN ANIMI DEMISSI MEMORIAM
P·D·C

In the great Cloister, on the pillar between one large window and another, are several frescoes by unknown artists; each fresco was commissioned on the occasion of the election of the Olivetan Abbot General or to record the visit of dignitaries.

D · O · M
REM OLIVETANAM
CYPRIANO VERONÊSI DOC
TRINA.ET EXIMIA.MORV̅ IN
TEGRITATIS VIRO.MODERÃE
CAROLVS IMPATORVEX
AFRICA,TVNETE DEBELIA
TA,VICTOR REGRESS.°, VTE̅
GA ITALIÆ.DISSIDIA PACE
CÔPESCERET, ÎSVBRIÃ PETS
BELLV̅ GALLIS ILLATVRVS
AƆVENERABILIS HVI°Æ.DIS
PIE RE INVISÊDÃ ACCESSI
EADÊQ.HVMILI MONACHOR
OBSEQO,ET FRVGALITAE.CC
TÊ.T.° HAVD IIVCVDE,VNI.
CA.NOCE HOSPITIO VS°.E.
IX.KA.MAIA.1536.
A PVERPERA VIRGINE.
CÔGRVV̅ SANE OMEN,
VT,QVI,IVRGIOP,POST DILV
VIEM,AƆPACÊ ERAT ARMATRAC
TATVR°.,PRI.° INTER COLVBAS,
ET SACRAS OLEAS REQESCERET.

Frescoes of the 14th century of the pilasters in the great Cloister.   *Frescoes of the 18th century.*

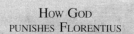

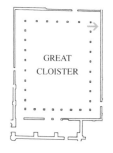

GREAT
CLOISTER

With this fresco, the first in the series by Signorelli, the story of St. Benedict continues chronologically. The group of monks are those we have seen departing with Benedict. The entire company has stopped to listen to a monk who has arrived running from Subiaco. Kneeling before Benedict, he relates that God has struck Florentius, causing his death under the ruins of his house which had suddenly collapsed shortly after the monks' departure, while Florentius was gloating over his victory on his terrace. They can therefore return. Benedict, whose face shows agitation and sorrow, answers that he will nonetheless continue his journey to Monte Cassino. Moreover, since the messenger appeared to him to have recounted their enemy's downfall with ill-disguised pleasure, Benedict reproves him and imposes a wholesome penance.

At also in the following frescoes by Signorelli, the original colors and hues have vanished under a single dull layer of spot, but out of this layer emerge some figures which express more than those of Sodoma those notes of recollection and austerity which are the hallmarks of Benedictine life.

Notice the manifest surprise on the faces of the monks, Florentius under the rubble, the four devils raging against the remains of the house to demolish them, the two devils carrying off the soul of the evil man, while a third strikes him.

How God punishes Florentius; detail.

This composition shows the first apostolic labours of Benedict and the Benedictines on Monte Cassino, which will see rise on its summit the world-renowned monastery.

In the center of the fresco, Benedict, assisted by two monks, teaches the first elements of Christian living to the region's inhabitants, still pagan. On the right in the background, a group of monks are occupied in pulling down the idol of Apollo, still worshipped locally. It may be useful to make a comparison between this fresco and that of Sodoma which depicts the evangelization of the peasants on Subiaco.

There is much more severity and religious spirit to in Signorelli's. The monks pulling down the statue of Apollo is a most successful aspect.

HOW BENEDICT EVANGELIZES
THE INHABITANTS
OF MONTE CASSINO

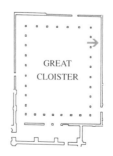

GREAT
CLOISTER

HOW BENEDICT DRIVES THE ENEMY FROM THE STONE

GREAT CLOISTER

St. Grègory the Great relates that the evil spirit continued to harass Benedict and his work in various ways. At times he would render immovable some blocks of stone which were needed for the construction; at other times, he would knock down part of what had already been built.

This fresco records one of those episodes of diabolical interference. In the center of the composition, a group of monks who, after vainly tiring themselves in their efforts to move a large stone which some strange force has rendered immovable, finally succeed in moving the stone as soon as Benedict traces the sign of the cross over it. On the right is a false fire, which four monks are bustling about, trying to put out.

On the left, the digging up of an idol. All three scenes are full of accuracy and life.

This is the fresco that completes the story of that war waged against Benedict by the devil. While a young monk is engaged in laying bricks on the top of wall, the devil causes a section of it to collapse, and with it the boy is dashed to the ground. His distressed fellow-monks pick him up and carry him to Benedict, who brings the youth back to life with his blessing.

Notice in the background on the left, how much realism there is in the figures of the two monks and the flapping of their habits as they seek shelter from the stones and boards that have fallen with the youth. Note also the sorrowful agitation of the monks who have picked up the corpse, as well as their awe-struck joy on the revival of the dead monk. Benedict is always surrounded by austere serenity.

HOW BENEDICT REVIVES
A YOUNG MONK ON WHOM
A WALL HAD FALLEN

GREAT CLOISTER

*How Benedict
tells the monks
where and when they had
eaten outside the monastery;
detail of a woman who pours
out the wine.*

*How Benedict
tells the monks
where and when they had
eaten outside the monastery;
detail.*

HOW BENEDICT TELLS THE
MONKS WHERE AND WHEN
THEY HAD EATEN OUTSIDE
THE MONASTERY

A meal taken by two monks in the modest home of some friendly people. In the Rule, Benedict had commanded that no one should eat outside of the monastery without permission. On returning, the unsuspecting monks are asked where they have eaten. "Nowhere", they answer. Benedict then proceeds to tell them with every precision of detail where and what they had eaten and drunk. The two religious, exposed, kneel before the saint and humbly ask forgiveness. The fresco, greatly deteriorated, has some figures which are perfect.

Particularly successful are the two women serving at table. The scene receives movement from the women in the background and from the young man in the doorway. To the right on top, the repentant monks being corrected.

The brother of the monk Valentinian, (mistakenly called Valerian), had the practice of going once a year fasting to Monte Cassino. This time, however, he has broken his fast, yielding to the insistence of a wayfarer he had met on the road. Benedict, after the first exchange of greetings, gently reproves him for having violated his fast. The shamed youth asks pardon on his knees. The three parts of the episode are treated with perfection. On the right, the young traveller and his unknown companion, whom the artist has depicted as horned, lame and slovenly dressed, so as to symbolize the tempting devil. On the left in the background, the two wayfarers intent on refreshing themselves by a spring; in the foreground, Benedict grants the young man the pardon he has requested.

How Benedict reproves the brother of the monk Valerian for having violated his fast

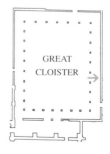

GREAT CLOISTER

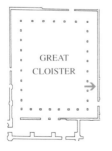

HOW BENEDICT EXPOSES TOTILA'S SHAM

GREAT CLOISTER

This fresco and the following complete one another.

Totila, the king of the Goths, during his incursions in Campania, has heard of Benedict , as being a man of God, and he decides to put to test the truth of this reputation.

He sends his shieldbearer Riggo, disguised as himself, to pay homage to Benedict. For if the latter does not perceive the deception, he will have every reason to disbelieve what the all too gullible people are saying. But as soon as the shieldbearer, disguised as Totila and accompanied by the royal entourage, appears before Benedict, the latter, to the astonishment and awe of monks and soldiers alike says to him: «Put off, o son, put off that garb that you are wearing; it is not your own». Riggo, on his knees with his arms open and his body contracted, could not better express awe and fright, and if some word were to issue from his mouth, it could be only a plea for compassion and mercy.

Pass again, one by one, the figures of the soldiers and the monks. Notice the variety in the way their astonishment is expressed, and what realism in their features. Delicate and dignified those of the monks, strong and coarse those of the soldiers. Benedict appears always austere and fatherly in his facial expression, resolute in the hand pointed at Riggo. The scene above is full of movement which shows Riggo after his return to the camp site, at the moment of relating to Totila what has taken place.

Riggo after his return to the camp site; detail.

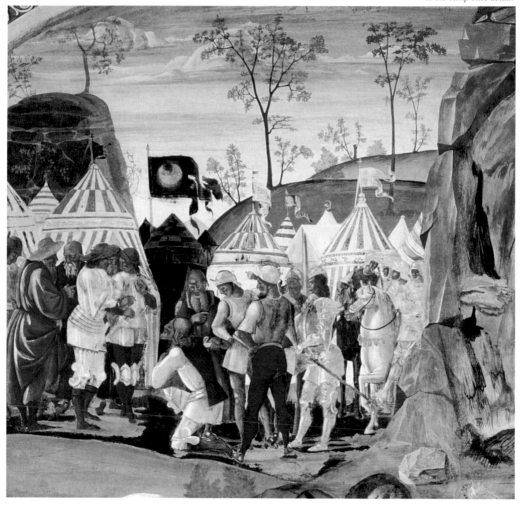

HOW BENEDICT RECOGNIZES AND RECEIVES TOTILA

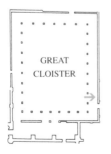

This fresco, which integrates with the previous one, is unfortunately the last of the series by Signorelli. Here we have Totila himself who, to make amends for the sham, has come in person to present Benedict his homages. The latter, who knows that he has before him the King of the Goths, stands leaning forward to raise up Totila, who has knelt and extended Benedict his hand. A marked coarseness is evident on the faces of the old warriors, an almost feminine softness on the faces of the young men. More than in the previous composition, there is grandeur and variety in the composition. In a scene substantially identical with the previous one, Signorelli has introduced so many new particulars, that this alone would suffice to show the fertility of his genius. Notice how well the four horsemen talking among themselves above express the violent traits of the soldiers in the service of the barbarian king.

How Benedict recognizes and receives Totila; detail of the soldiers.

HOW BENEDICT FORETELLS THE DESTRUCTION OF MONTE CASSINO

GREAT CLOISTER

We find ourselves before a new series of frescoes by Sodoma. This composition shows the destruction of Monte Cassino, prophesied by Benedict with tears in his eyes to a nobleman called Theoprobus on a visit of his to the monastery. Historically Monte Cassino was destroyed saveral times. The first time by the Longobards in 581. It is to this destruction that the pictorial representation alludes. After Signorelli's clear and measured scenes, this fresco by Sodoma with its great bivouac of powerful barbarians, their horses, solid and fierce, the devastation wrought on the monastery, gives the spirit a shock which tears it from its meditation and opens before it the vastness of an unexpected horizon, an horizon that follows Benedict's tragic prophecy by fifty years, and that epitomizes the fearful havoc that the iron and fire of the barbarians will make of Benedict's monumental work. Even though somewhat confused, the composition has a movement and a grandeur that give one the impression of standing before a masterpiece. Notice, in the group of barbarians, heads of horses and of men worthy of Leonardo da Vinci. To the right on top, is Benedict predicting the terrifying and vandalous devastation to Theoprobus.

How Benedict foretells the destruction of Monte Cassino; detail of the group of barbarians.

HOW BENEDICT OBTAINS FLOUR IN ABUNDANCE AND WITH IT RESTORES THE MONKS

This fresco, continuing the story of St. Benedict, shows his trust in Divine Providence.

It so happened, that since bread was becoming scarce, the monks began to manifest some trepidation for the future.

Benedict reproved them for having such little faith and promised that on the following day, they would have bread in abundance.

And so it happened, for on the next day, Providence caused two hundred *modii* of flour to be found at the door of the monastery.

On the right, the monks at table with Benedict.

We note on the table five small loaves and a few fish. Whether these represent the meal of the previous day or the meal with the bread sent by Providence, in either case, they bring to mind the five loaves and the few fishes that our Lord multiplied in the wilderness.

On the left is a lovely hall, with Benedict showing the abundant suply of flour to some of his astonished monks.

In describing the monastic refectory, the artist has omitted nothing. To the right in the pulpit, the reader who, according to the Rule, accompanies the monk's meals.

In the center, a beautiful crucifix, with the Virgin Mary and St. John.

After the tragic event recorded in the preceding fresco how much peace and serenity we find in these two scenes, illuminated by monastic faith and Divine Providence!

Observe the remarkable perspective and the effect of optical illusion produced by the monastic table. Its measurements reveal that it is a sort of trapezoid, which no one at first sight would suspect.

Also worthy of note are the two monks, the first two towards the spectator. One has taken his companion's bread, and the other, who with his raised hand says clearly that he is not disposed to part with it, shows surprise on his face. In front, the monk who is serving and notices everything smiles.

How Benedict obtains flour in abundance and with it restores the monks; detail of the table.

How Benedict appears to two
far-off monks and shows
them the design for the
construction of a monastery

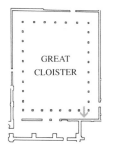

GREAT
CLOISTER

St. Gregory relates that Benedict, at the request of a gentleman of Terracina, sends some monks there to build a monastery, adding that he will come himself to show them how they must carry out the construction. One night, he appears to the superior of the new monastery and to his companion in a dream, and imparts the necessary instructions to them.

On the left, very expressive, the sleeping monks. To the right, a great deal of variety and life in the builders of the new monastery.

The landscape is beautiful. Noteworthy is the Latin inscription on the dormitory wall: *Sit nox cum somno et sine lite dies,* which means: "Let the night be with sleep and the day without contention". In the monk with the plumb-weight, we

SIT NOX CV̄ SONO
SIT SINE LITE DIES

Detail.

have the supposed portrait of the Olivetan architect, wood inlayer and sculptor, Fra Giovanni of Verona, at that time in Mount Olivet to inlay the choir.

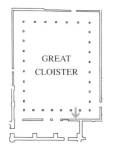

Two consecrated virgins, living in their own home, had received a stern admonition from Benedict, to amend themselves from the ugly vice they had of insulting a hired man, employed in the service of their noble house, with their rude and contemptuous language. Loquacious and stubborn as they were, however, they kept up their ugly habit. On their death they are buried in church. At that point where the deacon chants: «If there be anyone excommunicated, let him leave», a woman who had been the nurse of the two deceased, sees them leave their grave. Frightened and mindful of Benedict's reproach of the two religious when they were alive, she goes and informs him of what she has seen. Benedict gives the woman an alms to offer for the peace of the deceased, and the two immediately find peace in the grave. On the left, the two religious, leaving the tomb; in the center on top, solemn high mass; in front the people attending the mass. One of the better details, artistically, is the group of cantors. The two children playing, one with a little dog, the other with the dress of one of the women in the congregation are very delicately formed.

The child playing with a little dog; detail.

Group of cantors; detail.

A young monk had gone to visit his parents without Benedict's blessing. The monk died and was buried , but for two successive days afterwards, his corpse was found above ground. His relatives think of advising Benedict, who orders the Blessed Sacrament to be placed on the dead man's chest.

Thus his body finds peace in the grave.

The scene is a churchyard. On the right Benedict hands the monstrance containing the Sacred Host to a priest. In front, the priest placing the Blessed Sacrament on the body of the deceased. The appearance of the laymen taking part in the ceremony is full of energy, the faces of the altar boys assisting at the rite are very delicate, and the figure of the priest appears austere and collected.

Since a young monk kept insisting that he wanted to return to the life of the world, Benedict encouraged him on various occasions to persevere in that life he had vowed to God. Since the monk persists in his decision, however, Benedict finally permits him to leave. As soon as he is out of the monastery, the monk sees a terrifying monster coming towards him. He returns to the monastery, and seeing in this a sign from Heaven, he asks Benedict pardon, and zealously continues in the religious life which he has undertaken. The episode is treated realistically and with great expressiveness. On the right, the monk encountering the serpent. The terror that consumes him is evident on his face and in his bearing. On the left, Benedict with a group of monks receives the repentant youth on his return. They form a fascinating

HOW BENEDICT PARDONS THE MONK WHO, WISHING TO FLEE FROM THE MONASTERY, ENCOUNTERS A SERPENT ALONG THE ROAD

GREAT CLOISTER

group in their eloquent faces and gestures. An expression of severity and mercy in Benedict, sorrow and contrition in the offender, compassion and entreaty in the onlookers. Notice the beard that is disappearing in the monk near Benedict; it was not executed in fresco, but subsequently in tempera out of contempt for the monk here portrayed by Sodoma.

How Benedict releases a peasant who was bound by only looking at him; detail.

How Benedict releases a peasant who was bound, by only looking at him

This is the last fresco of the Signorelli-Sodoma cycle at Mount Olivet.

A cruel Goth by the name of Zalla captures a poor peasant, and threatens him with his life if he refuses to hand over all the money he owns. To save himself, the peasant says that he has consigned it all to Benedict. With that, the Goth compels the poor man to lead him at once to the man of God. Here, on their arrival, they find Benedict sitting at the monastery door, intent on reading. Zalla, with a haughty air, shouts that Benedict must give him the peasant's money. Benedict raises his eyes from the book, looks first at the Goth, then at the peasant, and the ropes that bind the latter fall at once

from his hands. The Goth, terrified by the prodigy, releases his prey and humbly accepts from Benedict the monition to be less cruel.

This fresco is unfortunately one of the most damaged. Still, what remains tells of its originality and perfection.

Especially well-preserved is the figure of the fierce Goth and also that of the peasant, quivering with terror.

This episode is a single note in the great hymn of gratitude which a humanity, harassed and afflicted, will have to raise throughout the Middle Ages to the Patriarch of Monks. For it was in the name of St. Benedict and following his example, that every Benedictine abbey became a refuge for all those persecuted by the arrogance and cruelty of barbarians and civilized men alike.

HOW BENEDICT RELEASES A PEASANT WHO WAS BOUND, BY ONLY LOOKING AT HIM

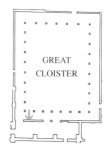

GREAT CLOISTER

Jesus Carrying the Cross.

OTHER FRESCOES BY SODOMA

In the same cloister, Sodoma's brush has left other frescoes of value.

On the walls of the arch which leads into the *Chapter* and from here to the church, one facing the other, are two small frescoes of a remarkable effectiveness.

On the left, *Jesus Carrying the Cross*.

The beautiful thorn-crowned head, the face stained by great dark drops of blood, the suffering of his humanity veiled by a serene melancholy, the bare flesh that bears the marks of the recent scourging, the soft hair falling on his shoulders, every detail shows the reality of an infinite suffering borne with infinite serenity. Completing the picture and giving it background and relief, is the figure of the executioner at our Saviour's shoulders, his eyes menacing, his brow furrowed, his teeth locked tight, is cane brutally goading on the Divine Sufferer.

The body of Christ, beautifully done, is clearly oppressed by the weight of the two massive beams of the cross.

Beneath, the legend: *Frangor maestitia premit intolerabile pondus; aggravat is cuius crimina pendo mala* "I am overcome by sadness, an unbearable weight oppresses me; it is rendered greater still by him whose great crimes I bear".

On the right, *Jesus at the Pillar*, preserved much better than the other. We are before a body virile and delicate, executed with that perfection we find only in Sodoma's masterpieces.

For the sake of comparison, let me remind you of the *St. Sebastian* at the Uffizi in Florence, as well as the

Scourging at the Pillar in the National Gallery of Siena. The body is so realistic, that it seems permeated with life. The bruises and the drops of blood, while they subtract nothing from the grace of the forms, call to mind the lashes

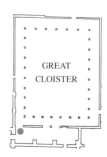

Jesus at the Pillar.

GREAT CLOISTER

which that delicate body has already received and will continue to receive. The head beautiful in its dilated eyes, in its half-opened mouth and in its unkempt hair, perfectly expresses suffering and resignation.

Another fine particular is the swelling of the flesh under the pressure of the rope.

Below, the legend: *Obsecro fixa meum speculentur*

Fathers of the Desert. Frescoes (1440) attributed to Giovanni di Paolo.

Madonna and Child. Marble sculpture of 1490.

Christ Ascending to Calvary.
Fresco by Bartolomeo Neroni
called Il Riccio (16th cent.).

lumina vultum, vestra quibus nostro est sanguine parta salus "O let your eyes stay to behold my face, o you, whom my blood has redeemed".

From the great Cloister - having crossed the corridor which originally constituted the second church of Monte Oliveto, and later the monastic cemetery, even today called *De profundis* - one enters the monastic church.

This place is also called the *Chapter* after the gatherings or *chapters* which were held there by the monks to pray for the souls of their deceased confrères.

On the walls of this corridor are remains of frescoes representing Fathers of the Desert, dated 1440, and attributed to Giovanni di Paolo.

In a niche, a delicate and majestic marble sculpture representing the Madonna and Child, attributed by some to the Olivetan fra Giovanni of Verona, and by others to the workshop of Mino of Fiesole.

To the side of the stairs a fresco by Bartolomeo Neroni called Riccio, representing *Christ ascending to Calvary.* On the other side of the great Cloister is another fresco by Sodoma representing the *Coronation of the Virgin.*

THE GREGORIAN CHANT

All people visiting Mount Oliveto are fascinated by the monks' Gregorian Chant, which leads you to experience unparalleled feelings. Through it, you long for God and spiritual values, your body and heart seem to reach a perfect peace.

The Gregorian Chant attracts both believers and unbelievers. Its origins date back to the early history of the Catholic Church. Pope St. Gregory the Great (604) reformed and codified the liturgical music, which was named after him. The golden era of the Gregorian Chant lasted between the 8th and the 13th century. After a difficult period of some neglect, its original purity was resumed by Abbot Guéranger and Solesmes monks (France). Vatican Council II acknowledged it as a distinctive feature of Roman Liturgy and fostered its use during liturgical events.

The Gregorian Chant has a modal style, including more than 2100 modulations. This is the main reason for the spiritual feelings experienced by singers as well as the audience. Antoine de Saint-Exupéry wrote that "There's no problem: if you can rain down on men something like the Gregorian Chant". In Mount Oliveto's abbey and other Benedictine monasteries, the Gregorian Chant is sung during the Mass, the Vespers, the "Compietà" and, partially, during the Lauds and the Minor Hours.

Page of an illuminated choral book with the representation of Pentecost (15th cent.).

The church was built between the years 1400 and 1417, according to a Gothic-Romanesque plan. In 1772, however, its elegant and majestic Gothic simplicity had to yield to the ascendant baroque. The architect was Giovanni Antinori of Came-rino. On the outside, he spared the campanile and the entrance door, and on the interior - in the form of a Latin cross - he lavished cornices, ornaments, columns, capital and a *gloria* of angels in the apse.

The entire long arm is occupied by the magnificient choir, carved and inlaid by fra Giovanni of Verona, the most renowned of Olivetan artists in woodcarving and inlay work. In all, the choir is made up of 125 stalls, distributed in double rows, two lower with 58 stalls, and two upper with 67. Only 48,

however, are inlaid. The stalls are separated one from another diversely and finely sculpted; they are bordered above and below by arabesques in miniature, and the whole forms a monumental artistic block with an inlaid, yellow and blue painted ceiling.

It is impossible to describe in writing the beauty of each individual stall, and of the whole unit. In each and every choir stall, there are

THE CHURCH

*Interior of the abbey church
with the great inlaid choir
(1503-1505) by Fra Giovanni of Verona.*

Cup of a censer, incense-boat.

Musical instruments.

View of the Colosseum.

Vase of flowers, dodecahedron and books.

landscapes, sacred vessels, birds, musical instruments, towns on mountain-sides, music rolls, all presented

with such grace and harmony, originality and realism, grandeur and beauty of colour, that you think you are

View of Verona's street.

Landscape.

Saint Benedict.

looking at a painting.
In the middle of the choir,
rises a massive lectern by the
Olivetan inlayer, Fra Raffae-

Flutes, lute and score.

The Palazzo Pubblico of Siena.

Lectern (1520) by Fra Raffaele of Brescia.

Intarsia of the lectern; detail.

le of Brescia. It is dated 1520, and is characterized by an almost life-size cat under an arcade in perspective.

Other works of art worthy of note are: the fresco representing the Founder of Mount Olivet with his two first companions, by an unknown artist; the large painting above the high altar, showing the *Birth of the Virgin Mary*, painted in 1598 by Jacopo Ligozzi, a disciple of Paolo Veronese, to replace an identical painting by the same Ligozzi, which had been moved to the Grand Duke of Tuscany (the latter having requested it for the Infanta Isabel of Spain as a

*Birth
and Assumption
of the Virgin,
by Jacopo Ligozzi
(16th cent.).*

gift on their wedding day); a lovely painting of the *Assumption* by the same artist, placed high in the center of the cross-vault; the two frescoes by Francesco Vanni on the sides of the transept, representing the *Consecration of the Church*, and the religious *Investiture of the first Olivetans*; the *Silver Ladder* (here depicted as

*Consecration
of the Church
and Investiture
of the first Olivetans,
by Francesco Vanni (16th cent.).*

Annunciation (17th cent.).

*St. Benedict appears
to Blessed Bernard Tolomei.
Painting over the left side altar (17th cent.).*

a stairway) a fresco on the ceiling by Ermenegildo Costantini; the abbot's throne carved in cypress wood, well executed and in tune with the surroundings, a work of the Olivetan monk, Dom Benoît M. Constantin (1948); and the *stained-glass windows* by Lino Dinetto (1965 and 1972).

To the sides of the sanctuary, there are three chapels. The

*The Infant Mary
(18th cent.).*

one on the right, on whose vault is a lovely 17th-century roundel in oil of the *Annunciation*, is dedicated to St. Frances of Rome; the one on the left to Blessed Bernard Tolomei, and beyond the door in the left wall of the church, the chapel dedicated to Christ Crucified.

Worthy of note: in the chapel of Blessed Bernard Tolomei, is a lovely image of the *Infant Mary* in an artistic glass-covered case; in the chapel of the Crucified, a large *Crucifix* in wood, both artistic and devotional, which was brought here by the Founder of Mount Olivet in 1313, and which, according to the Olivetan chronicle, spoke to the saint several times.

Expressive and devout is the figure of Blessed Bernard, painted at the foot of the Crucifix by Raffaele Vanni. Though the invading French under Napoleon stripped the sacristy of its vestments and

The Chapel of Christ Crucified.

The Crucifix who spoke to the saint Bernard Tolomei.

sacred vessels from the past, it still conserves an artistic note in the beautiful, finely inlaid vestment tables along the walls, dating from the year 1417. The Gothic ceiling and the fifteenth century fillet form a characteristic and picturesque whole, notwithstanding the disparity of intonation given by elements of different periods up to the baroque of the medallions.

View of the sacristy.

*The Coronation
of the Virgin
by Sodoma.*

THE
LIBRARY

*Stairs leading
to the library.*

At Monte Oliveto Maggiore, as in all Benedictine abbeys, the library was not only important, but constructed along monumental lines, it was enabled to contain a vast amount of books.

We approach up two flights of stairs in travertine. One flight is as old as the monastery itself. It rises from the ground floor between the great cloister and the middle cloister in front of the wrought-iron gate that marks the clausura, and brings us up to the first floor. Climbing a few more steps to the right, we find a double semicircular ramp, of recent construction, which takes us up to the entrance-hall of the library. Half-way up the first flight, a fresco by Sodoma, unfortunately deteriorated, shows the *Coronation of the Virgin Mary*, with a Latin inscription that invites us to bend our knee before Mother

Library door.

and Son. At the top of the second flight, there are some frescoes dating from the seventeeth century, by the Olivetan, Antonius Müller of Danzig. They depict Blessed Bernard's vision, bishops, abbots general, illustrious persons and the accomplishments of three Olivetan cardinals, Pietro Tartaro, Giorgio Martinusio and Ardicino della Porta. The magnificient Paschal candlestick by Fra Giovanni of Verona brings the visitor back to the early years of Mount Olivet. Mount Olivet's library was built in the years 1513 and 1514, while Francesco Ringhieri of Bologna was Abbot General. Architect was Fra Giovanni of Verona himself, who carved the capitals for the columns out of pietra serena with his own hand, and also carved the magnificient entrance door, besides the already mentioned Paschal candlestick, and a magnificient cabinet for choral books.

The great mass of books which the library once contained, among which manuscripts and incunabula of rare value, and a *Divine Comedy* translated into Latin verses by the Olivetan, Matteo Ronto, is today scattered throughout the world, and the

Interior of the library.

*Details of
illuminated choral books (15th cent.):
The Resurrection;
The introits of Christmas Day Mass;
King David playing the harp;
The Adoration of the Magi.*

*A cupboard inlayed,
Fra Giovanni of Verona.*

precious volumes, parchments and documents that cost the monks of Mount Olivet so much fatigue and expense, adorn and enrich various public and private libraries. Even the ancient *plutei* have disappered.

The illuminated choral books, created specially by the monks of Mount Olivet, and even more precious, were removed and are today in the cathedral of Chiusi. Some years ago, to fill up somehow the desolate void, twenty illuminated choral books of the 15th and 16th centuries, belonging to the suppressed Olivetan monastery of Monte Morcino at Perugia, had been arranged in artistic show-cases. Unfortunately, even these, some of which are illustrated here, together with a lavish collection of old coins, have been the object of numerous thefts at the abbey in recent years.

THE CENTRAL CLOISTER

It was erected in the 15th century using mixed severe and gentle lines with is graceful little loggia facing south.

Above the entrance door, shaped like a half-moon, there is a *Madonna with Child* of the 15th century.

The fresco with its artistical brick frame was discovered in 1972 by removing the fresco of the great Cloister on the opposite side.

The fresco was accompanied by a parchment written in Latin with Indian ink, which said: «This Madonna has been covered by Sodoma in order to continue his series of

View of the central Cloister.

frescos about St. Benedict, though in these times she has already worked many wonders».

This parchment is now preserved in the archives of the abbey.

Madonna with Child and Angels (15th cent.).

View of the little Cloister.

The monastic life is so strange and mysterious for laymen, that the visitor is interested in all its particulars.

It is no wonder, for instance, that even in monasteries, there are plates and pottery for the everyday meals. Well, in the great refectory of Mount Olivet, even this understandable curiosity of yours will be satisfied. On the long cypres-wood tables, you can admire a row of the traditional crockery used for the monastic meals.

In the entrance-hall, a lovely lavabo in yellow Senese marble.

Built between the years 1387 and 1390, under the Abbots General Ducco Bertolini of Arezzo and Ippolito of Milan, artistically decorated refectory, unfortunately, bears the marks of devastation. Still, its vastness and its decoration may offer you a few things that merit attention and that will leave you with some pleasant memories.

A large fresco on the back wall representing the *Last Supper*, in the little that remains of it, shows part of a table cloth and the bust of an apostle. It is probably from the school of Ghirlandaio.

Its place has been taken by a *Last Supper* on canvas by Lino Dinetto (1948).

On the ceiling, and along part of the walls, frescoes of the seventeenth century represent events from Old Testament, Sybils and allegorical figures.

They are the work of Fra Paolo of Alfidena, an Olivetan oblate, who says of his work that it was fruit not of his talent, but only of obedience.

THE REFECTORY

View of the refectory.

*The apse
and the bell-tower
of the abbey church.*

FAREWELL

*Do not leave without first
having given yourself
the pleasure of a pause
in the welcoming shade
of the cypresses.*

*The chapel of
St. Bernard Tolomei.*

Along this path there are two chapels, and a third above to the right, towards the Tower. The first chapel is dedicated to the founder of Mount Olivet, and rises over the grotto where for years he lived, withdrawn in prayer and penance.

The present construction goes back to 1760. On the vault, a fresco by Apollonio Nasini recalls the numerous victories Blessed Bernard won over the evil spirits with the powerful aid of the Archangel Michael. On the sides, four plaster statues by Scutellari of Bologna (1763), and above the altar, a painting by Stefano Pozzo of Milan complete the chapel, which is built around the authentic grotto. The grotto itself is covered with marble, and

Loggia (15th cent.).

dominated by a ceramic statue of Blessed Bernard, in the place of the original marble one sculptured by Pasquale Boccardi of Genoa.

The devout have a custom of bringing back with them a bit of earth from this grotto.

The chapel of St. Scholastica, at the end of the path, was built in the early days of Mount Olivet, but has been variously altered in the course of the centuries. In the apse it preserves a precious fresco by Fra Antonio of Bologna, an Olivetan lay brother (1515). It represents the *Assumption of the Virgin* amid a *gloria* of angels. The chapel of St. Frances of Rome (1644), with a few others, which have recently been restored, complete our tour. If you like, before you leave, climb the

The octagonal chapel of St. Francis of Rome.

hill that dominates the whole of Mount Olivet to the southeast. You will bring away with you memory of the the whole magnificient and picturesque panorama.

THE MONASTERY OF ST. NAZARIO: THE BENEDICTINE OLIVETAN NUNS

Tourists coming from Buoncovento along a road crossing a variety of small valleys and hills, are struck by silver olive trees and vineyard shades, by typical Sienna colour and the granitic red of fired bricks, faded by time, of a group of cottages. Four kilometres before Mount Oliveto, the convent of a community of Benedictine olivetan nuns stands on a rise to the right, reaching a ring of mountains: St. Nazario.

Founded in 1955, in buildings located near an ancient, recently restored, Roman parish, it is the spiritual "outpost" of the large abbey nearby. Nuns pay homage to Gods supremacy with joy and simplicity, by following St. Benedicts rule with energy and vitality and planning their life according to the famous saying *ora et labora*. Daily bread is assured by several manual activities, such as the sewing and embroidery laboratory - producing works of art ! - and farm works in the small field around the monastery. Embroideries are made to order (phone : 0577/707018) or reaching an agreement with the Prioress in the monastery parlour. Small guest-rooms are at the disposal of all girls interested in experiencing monastic life.

Address :
Monastero Monache
Benedettine Olivetane
San Nazario
53020 Chiusure (Siena)